I0139960

**Next Steps: Infinite Possibilities and Enlightenment**

**ISBN-10**:978-1-7341346-1-2

**LOC#:** 2020905825

Copyright @ Shawn C. Foster

**Publisher, Editor and Graphics**:

Fiery Beacon Publishing House

Greensboro, N.C.

# NEXT STEPS:

# INFINITE POSSIBILITIES AND ENLIGHTENMENT

## BY SHAWN C. FOSTER

## ACKNOWLEDGEMENTS

*My Family*

*My Elim Christian Fellowship Family*

*My Sisterhood - Free Women In Christ – Outreach Ministries*

*Thank God for everything!*

# INTRODUCTION

TODAY, IN OUR ADULT LIVES, GRACE COMES TO US IN MANY SHAPES AND FORMS. MOST OF ALL, GRACE IS THE GIFT OF GOD'S UNCONDITIONAL LOVE. SOME DAYS WE GET SO BUSY THAT WE FORGET TO SEE THE GIFTS OF GRACE THAT FILLS OUR LIVES. BUT GOD'S GRACE IS ALWAYS THERE, WAITING TO BE ENJOYED.

NOT A SOMETIMES THING; IT IS AN "ALL THE TIME" THING! WHEN WE MAKE PRAYER A PRIORITY EVERY DAY, WE KEEP THE LINES OF COMMUNICATION OPEN BETWEEN GOD AND OURSELVES ALL THROUGH THE DAY, MOMENT BY MOMENT, STEP BY STEP.

NEXT STEPS WILL HELP US TO NOTICE THE MANY GIFTS THAT GOD GRACES US WITH.  NEXT STEPS WILL HELP YOU GAIN INSIGHT THAT IS RELEVANT.  THERE ARE ACTIONABLE TIPS STRAIGHT FROM THE WORD OF GOD TO KEEP YOU FOCUSED WITH GUIDANCE, ADVICE AND ENCOURAGEMENT WHILE HOLDING YOU ACCOUNTABLE TO THE ACTIONS YOU MUST TAKE.

WE INDIVIDUALLY AND COLLECTIVELY CHOOSE TO RELEASE REGRETS OF THE PAST.

WHAT WE DO TODAY CREATES OUR TOMORROW

–

PREPARE YOURSELF!

MAY YOU KNOW PEACE
AND STAY HIGHLY
MOTIVATED!

# PONDER THE ISSUES AND ALLOW GOD TO REVEAL HIS TRUTH TO YOU!

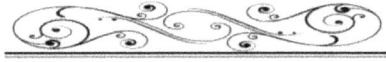

EVERY MORNING AND
NIGHT

GET ON YOUR KNEES

PRAY A BLESSING
OVER YOUR DAY

AND THANK GOD FOR
IT ALL!

FIND A WAY TO GET
SOME ASSISTANCE
TO SOMEONE IN
NEED – MAKE IT A
LIFE MISSION AND
FOLLOW THROUGH.

# FIND A PASSAGE AND MEMORIZE IT!

## ROMANS 3:3-5; 12:12

## LAMENTATIONS 3:21-23, 25

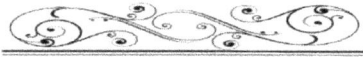

# SPEAK LIFE!

## CHALLENGE YOURSELF TO SPEAK FAITH OVER EVERY CHALLENGE IN YOUR LIFE REGARDLESS OF WHAT IT LOOKS OR FEELS LIKE!

WRITE DOWN AN
IMMEDIATE NEED,
ASK GOD TO SUPPLY
THIS NEED AND
THANK HIM FOR
MEETING THE NEED!

HELP ME LORD TO
BE WHAT YOU WANT
ME TO BE!

HOW CAN I PRAY
FOR YOU?

SAY IT WITH ME:

I (YOUR NAME) AM A
CHILD OF GOD
BECAUSE HE SAID
SO!

# TRUST GOD!

# GOD'S MANDATE FOR ME IS TO LEAD OTHERS TO DO GOOD!

PRAY THE PRAYER OF
FAITH!

PHILIPPIANS 4:19

FILL YOUR FAITH BANK
ACCOUNT.

BELIEVE GOD TO
PROVIDE FOR YOUR
IMMEDIATE NEED.
THANK HIM FOR THE
MANIFESTATION!

# THANK GOD FOR HELPING TO ENSURE THAT OUR FAITH STAYS STRONG!

## PRAY FIRST, THEN ACT!

## ASK THE LORD OF THE HARVEST TO HELP YOU BRING OTHERS TO CHRIST.

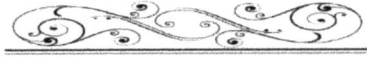

# KNOW THAT WE HAVE AN ADVOCATE WHO IS STILL WORKING IN OUR BEST INTEREST!

# COMMIT TO BECOMING A RESERVOIR OF HOPE!

## THINK IT.

## PRAY IT.

TAKE WHAT YOU
HAVE LEARNED
TODAY AND DO
SOMETHING ABOUT
IT.

# THIS WEEK PLAN FOR THE MOST IMPORTANT THINGS IN YOUR LIFE:

## TIME WITH GOD

## TIME WITH YOUR CHILDREN

## EXERCISE AND REST

## EATING HEALTHY AND RELAXATION

# PRAY THESE SCRIPTURES

## DEUTERONOMY 28: 1-14

## MATTHEW 5:1-11

## EPHESIANS 1:1-23

# PRAY DAILY!

# RECONNECT WITH GOD.

# RECOMMIT TO HIM.

# GOD'S WORD MUST BE OUR GUIDING PRINCIPLE.

DO NOT BE A PART
OF THE PROBLEM.

BE A PART OF THE
SOLUTION.

# LISTEN TO TODAY'S MESSAGE AGAIN OR ANY OTHER PREVIOUS MESSAGE ON

## RIGHT NOW MEDIA

## WWW.ELIMCF.ORG

# GOD WILL SUPPLY
# BUT WE MUST

# APPLY!

SEND A TEXT TO
SOMEONE AND
REMIND THEM THAT
THEY ARE MORE
THAN A
CONQUEROR!

# GO BACK TO THE FIRST PLACE YOU MET JESUS!

PREPARE FOR EACH
DAY WITH PRAYER
ASKING GOD TO GIVE
YOU A HUNGER AND
THIRST FOR RIGHT
LIVING.

DO THE RIGHT
THING!

# WE HAVE THE POWER.

# SPEAK LIFE!

# THIRST NO MORE!

## JOHN 4:14

# GOD WANTS TO REBUILD BUT THE PEOPLE MUST PARTICIPATE.

READ THE BIBLE.

GO TO LUNCH WITH
GOD.

WALK WITH GOD

TALK THROUGH
PRAYER WITH GOD!

# CHANGE YOUR THINKING TO CHANGE YOUR PERSPECTIVE.

# PLANNING, MEASURING, AND EXECUTING ARE CRITICAL TOOLS IN THE MANIFESTATION OF OUR BELIEFS!

EACH OF US MUST
MODEL INTEGRITY
IN THE MAKING AND
KEEPING OF OUR

COMMITMENTS.

"DON'T LIMIT YOUR
CHALLENGES,
INSTEAD
CHALLENGE YOUR
LIMITS."

-UNKNOWN

REMEMBER THAT
EVERYONE YOU CAN
COUNT, CANNOT BE
COUNTED ON.

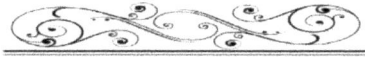

YOUR INITIATIVE
WILL INITIATE
DIVINE
INTERVENTION ON
YOUR BEHALF.

ONE OF LIFE'S
GREATEST
CHALLENGES IS
LEARNING HOW TO
DEAL WITH THINGS
THAT GOD MAY NOT
CHANGE.

# DO NOT SETTLE FOR MARGINALITY!

# GET READY FOR BREAKTHROUGH!

# REMEMBER HIS SACRIFICE ON THE CROSS FOR YOU!

EACH WEEK SET
ASIDE AN OFFERING
ACCORDING TO WHAT
YOU HAVE EARNED,
TO BRING TO THE
HOUSE OF GOD!

BE FAITHFUL AND
PERSISTENT!

# FIND SOMEONE WHO DOES NOT KNOW GOD AND SHOW THEM THE GOODNESS OF GOD!

# THIS WEEK PAY CLOSE ATTENTION TO THE THINGS WE GIVE OUR HEARTS TO.

## PRAY AND SAY:

LORD HELP ME TO BE
OBEDIENT TO YOU
AND BE AVAILABLE
FOR YOU TO FILL ME
WITH YOUR HOLY
SPIRIT.

AMEN!

# PRAY FOR YOUR PASTOR!

# MEMORIZE THIS SCRIPTURE:

# PSALM 8:4-9

LET GOD PUT HIS
HANDS ON IT!

SUIT UP DAILY! ARMOR
UP DAILY!

PRAY THROUGH
EPH.6:10-18

HE WILL BE STRONG IN
YOU! PUT ON THE FULL
ARMOR!

# READ PSALM 23 TWO TO THREE TIMES A DAY!

ASK GOD TO TEACH
YOU TO PRAY
ACCORDING TO HIS
WILL AND EXPECT
HIM TO FILL YOUR
REQUEST.

ASK AND KEEP
ASKING!

SEEK AND KEEP
SEEKING!

KNOCK AND KEEP
KNOCKING!

# EXALT, EXTOL AND MAGNIFY GOD!

# RECEIVE HIS RIGHTEOUSNESS, JOY AND PEACE!

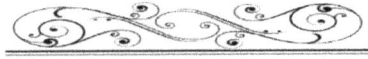

# PLAN OUT PRAYER TIMES THROUGHOUT THE DAY!

# LISTEN TO ONE INSPIRATIONAL MESSAGE DAILY!

HELP US LORD, TO
BE AN ANSWER TO
SOMEONE'S PRAYER
EVERY DAY THIS
WEEK.

LORD HELP ME TO FIND
MY DELIGHT IN YOU
AND LIVE FOR YOUR
GLORY ALONE!

MOVE IN OBEDIENCE.

"TRUST IN THE LORD
WITH ALL YOUR HEART
AND LEAN NOT ON
YOUR OWN
UNDERSTANDING; IN
ALL YOUR WAYS
ACKNOWLEDGE HIM.
"

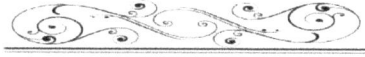

# PRACTICE ASKING:

## ONE-ON ONE WITH GOD
## OR

## WITH ANOTHER PERSON,

## FOR SOMETHING THAT IS ONLY POSSIBLE WITH GOD AND FOR BIGGER SITUATIONS.

**REFOCUS
SPIRITUALLY.**

**REFOCUS
MENTALLY.**

**REFOCUS
EMOTIONALLY!**

REPLACE ALL
NEGATIVE
THOUGHTS WITH
POSITIVE
SCRIPTURES.

ASK GOD FOR
PATIENCE.

# EMPOWER, HELP, ENCOURAGE AND STRENGTHEN SOMEONE ELSE!

DEDICATE THIS WEEK
TO BEING AN ANSWER
TO PRAYER BY
MEETING THE NEEDS
OF THE PEOPLE
AROUND YOU
ESPECIALLY THOSE
WHO YOU DO NOT
LIKE.

# SET YOUR MIND ON PLEASING GOD!

# NAME YOUR "THIS!"

# PRAISE GOD!

# FIND CREATIVE WAYS TO STRENGTHEN YOUR PARTNERSHIPS!

# FOR THE NEXT SEVEN DAYS PRAY:

## LORD PLEASE ALLOW YOUR LOVE TO LEAD ME TODAY!

# START A PRAYER JOURNAL!

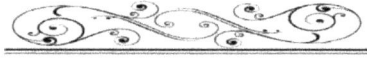

# SEVEN DAY DIET OF HOPE FILLED STRATEGIES:

## NEVER MAKE A DECISION WHEN YOU ARE DOWN, RESPOND TO BAD NEWS IN GOOD WAYS, AND SHAKE IT OFF AND STEP IT UP!

# THIS WEEK PICK A DAY TO DO NOTHING!

# MORNING, NOON AND NIGHT-

# PRAY!

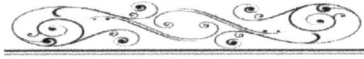

EACH OF US MUST
TAKE
RESPONSIBILITY FOR
OUR ACTIONS, OUR
WELL-BEING AND THE
ACQUISITION OF OUR
MAXIMUM
POTENTIAL!

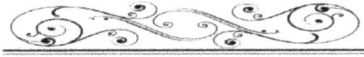

# INFLUENCE MORE LIVES!

WE HEIGHTEN OUR
OWN LIVES WHEN
WE HELP OTHERS
HEIGHTEN THEIRS.

# NOTES

# CONNECT WITH THE AUTHOR

Shawn C. Foster has spent a lifetime helping others overcome myriad life challenges, obstacles, and personal issues.

She is a best-selling Author, Child Care Provider, Librarian's Assistant, Early Childhood Professional, Entrepreneur, and Mother of 2 adult daughters, 3 grandsons, and 1 granddaughter.

Born in Baltimore, Maryland raised in Queens, New York and now resides in Greensboro, North Carolina. She says, "Instead of second-guessing yourself and wondering what to do next, just think!"

Next Steps: Infinite Possibilities and Enlightenment, will keep you in a positive mindset when it feels like the world is not "business as usual."  This book will provide you with instructions you will need to succeed on a daily basis. You can easily follow what the words say and LIVE an abundant LIFE!

### ***Stay Connected***

Email: scfoster88@yahoo.com

Telephone: 336.965.5552

Facebook: Shawn C. Foster

YouTube

Twitter: @ShawnCFoster1

www.ingramcontent.com/pod-product-compliance
Lightning Source LLC
Chambersburg PA
CBHW052203090426
42741CB00010B/2390